Shak's Indian Kitchen

SHAKUNTALA SHINDE

Photography by Dilip Shinde

www.popularprakashan.com

Published by
Harsha Bhatkal for
Popular Prakashan Pvt. Ltd.
301, Mahalaxmi Chambers
22, Bhulabhai Desai Road
Mumbai 400026
info@popularprakashan.com

© 2022 Shakuntala Shinde
First Published 2022

(4545)
ISBN 978-81-956688-4-7

WORLD RIGHTS RESERVED. The contents are original and copyrighted. No portion of this book shall be reproduced, stored in a retrieval system or transmitted by any means, electronic, mechanical, photocopying, recording or otherwise, without the written permission of the author and the publisher.

Photography: Dilip Shinde
Cover Design: PealiDezine
Inside Layouting: Anjali Sawant

Printed In India
by Print Plus Private Limited
212, Swastik Chambers, ST Road
Chembur, Mumbai 400071

*Dedicated to my beloved
mother and mother-in-law*

Foreword

It is truly heartening to see Ms. Shakuntala Shinde carry forward the tradition of Indian recipes with this book release.

I appreciate the sincere efforts that have gone into compiling the book which will serve as a good repertoire of her chosen recipes.

The book is a good effort towards helping lovers of Indian cuisine taste authentic homemade recipes without having to worry about 'calories'.

With this book, Ms. Shakuntala Shinde shares her much-loved recipes with her patrons. The Indian diaspora and food aficionados the world over will be benefited from this book that has Indian equivalent of English ingredients.

I wish her success and the very best in all her future endeavours.

God Bless!

— *Master Chef Sanjeev Kapoor*
Celebrity Chef, Best-selling Author,
Padma Shri awardee
& the Face of Indian Cuisine

Author's Note

I grew up in a very happy lower middle class Kannada family in Mumbai, with a "zest for life" and my parents ensured that food was never an issue. I grew up a foodie, who loved to try out "different tastes" and preparations from all over India. I married into a Maharashtrian family who further added to my palate more varieties than I had previously tasted. My mom and mother-in-law taught me a lot and really helped me develop a liking for cooking. We moved to USA in 1993, which exposed me to even more international cuisines.

I love to watch TV shows on cooking and reading cook-books. With God's grace, we have done well here in the USA. We moved to Pittsburgh in 1996 and have since made it our home. We soon got to know a large number of fun loving Indians and made a large number of close friends with whom we've had frequent parties. By 2004, our social life had prospered to such an extent that we would have 3 major parties at our home in a year with more than 75 attendees at each party, all with different groups of friends. This was in addition to multiple other smaller parties throughout the year with many very close friends. I took pride in cooking the entire menu for all my parties, including appetizers, main entrees and desserts. It gave me immense pleasure when the guests raved about my food, which motivated me to experiment even more with tasty dishes. I maintain a list of items served at each party to help ensure my guests taste new recipes with no repetitions.

During these years I started to write down my own recipes with quantities of ingredients properly measured as I wanted to ensure authentic replication of my dishes when I started getting multiple requests for my recipes. Initially these were recorded in a notebook. Many years ago, my husband and my biggest fan, convinced me to convert all the recipes to a digital format. My entire family enjoys my cooking and for many years they've wanted me to publish my recipes and occasionally even tried to convince me to open a restaurant. I was never enthused, until now, due to the hassles of publishing a book.

Last year in December we had two of our best friends, Drs. Ram and Meena Prabhoo, classmates of my husband, visit us from India. At one of the dinners, their praise for my food led to a conversation about the 250 plus recipes I had typed up on my computer. They insisted that I must author a cook-book with my recipes. They told us how they were able to help our world renowned chef, Sanjeev Kapoor publish some of his cook-books with the help of Harsha Bhatkal, Dr. Meena's cousin, who owns Popular Prakashan. My family was totally convinced. As soon as Dr. Ram realized my reluctant commitment, he called Harsha right away in India to set the ball rolling.

Writing this cook book became our "New Year's Resolution". I shortlisted 75 recipes consisting of both non-veg and veg appetizers and main entrees as well as desserts and cooked them over the next 4 months, almost one recipe a day. My husband then photographed them to the best of his (limited) ability. During this period, I had one of the best times of my life as I felt like a child who gets to play with her favorite toys.

Harsha and his team have worked diligently since then to publish this book for everyone's pleasure. As I'm known as SHAK here in USA, "Shak's Indian Kitchen", I believe, describes my book perfectly as it contains Indian recipes from my kitchen. The main reason, which convinced me to author this book, was to honor my husband's wish to record these recipes for posterity. I do not have any financial ambitions from this book. All I want is for my patrons to enjoy the "real" homemade recipes without much regard to "calories".

I will be happy to discuss, guide, and give additional tips to anyone who is interested in my recipes. Please send me an email at shaksindiankitchen@yahoo.com for any queries. Hope you all enjoy the recipes as much or even more than my family and friends do. ENJOY.

— *Shak Shinde*

Acknowlegements

Mom (Amma) Rajivi Rao

Mother in law (Aai) Sanjivani Shinde

Dr. Ram Prabhoo

Dr. Meena Prabhoo

Master Chef Sanjeev Kapoor

Abhishek Shinde

Ashwin Shinde

Morli Gandhi Shinde

Swarup Nemlekar

Contents

BREAKFAST

Medu Vada	12
Sambhar	15
Upma	16

APPETIZERS AND SNACKS

Batata Vada	18
Chakli	21
Corn Tikkis	22
Dal Vada	25
Fresh Salsa	26
Kothimbir Bhajji	27
Khandvi (Microwave)	29
Samosa	30
Seekh Kababs	32
SFC (Shak's Fried Chicken)	33
Shrimp or Prawn Pakora	34
Tandoori Chicken	35
Stuffed Mushrooms	36
Tuna Fish Cutlets	39
Broccoli Bake	40
Black Chana Chaat	42
Spinach Balls	43

VEGETARIAN DISHES

Kadhi Pakora	45
Zucchini Mushroom Stir Fry	46
Tondli Garlic Fry	47
Baingan Bhartha	48
Capsicum Aloo Sabzi	49
Black-eyed Peas Curry	50
Cabbage-Chana Dal Subzi	52
Mahki Dal	53
Chole	55
Palak Paneer	56
Corn Capsicum Masala	57
Matar Paneer	58
Dal Palak	60
Eggplant Bhaaji	61
Gobi Capsicum Masala	62
Karela (Bitter Gourd) Sabzi	63
Mushroom Masala	64
Palak Mushroom	66
Stuffed Okra (Bhindi)	67
Sprouted Moong Curry	69
Vegetable Korma	70
White Peas (Vatana) Curry	72
Whole Moong Dal	73

NON-VEGETARIAN DISHES

Amma's Chicken Curry	74
Bhuna Chicken	76
Chicken 65	77
Chettinad Mutton Curry	78
Chicken Biryani	80
Chicken Handi	83
Chicken-Liver Palak Masala	84
Crab Curry	87
Green Chicken	88
Kheema	89
Lamb Pepper Fry	90
Mutton Noval Kol Curry	93
Pomfret Fish Curry	94
Shrimp Sukka	96
Shrimp Capsicum Masala	97
Shrimp Curry (Shinde Style)	98
Mutton Rogan Josh	101

INDO-CHINESE DISHES

Chicken Manchow Soup	102
Chili Chicken (Indo-Chinese)	105
Fried Rice	106

DESSERTS

Banana Choc-chip Bread	108
Carrot Halwa	110
Doodhi (Bottle Gourd) Halwa	111
Date and Nut Roll	112
Pista Barfi	114
Ribbon Jell-O	116
Rava Kesari	117
Mango-Coconut Barfi	118

MASALAS

Chai Masala	120
Kadai Masala Powder	121
Sambhar Powder	122
Shinde Masala	123

Measurements	124
American and Indian Equivalents of Ingredients	124

Medu Vada

Ingredients

500 grams (18 oz) skinless split black gram (dhuli urad dal), thoroughly washed and soaked in water for 5-6 hours

Method:

- Drain all the water from the soaked skinless split black gram.
- Grind the dal in a blender or an idli grinder to a medium fine paste, using very little water (approximately ½ cup).
- Beat the batter well, using your hand, in one direction until it is fluffy and the color of the batter gets lighter.
- Heat oil in a deep fryer.
- Wet your fingers and the palms of your hands and make medu vadas with a hole in the center. You can also use a medu vada making machine.
- Deep fry the medu vadas in hot oil, on a medium high heat till medium brown in color.
- Drain on a paper towel.
- Serve with piping hot sambhar.

Serves 6-8 people

Chef's tip: Drop a pinch of the batter in a cup of water. If it floats, your batter is ready for making vadas. You could also use ¼ teaspoon of baking soda, mixed well in the batter for light, fluffy and crispy vadas. The art of making medu vadas with a hole in the center comes with practice. They say practice makes a woman perfect.

Sambhar

Ingredients

250 grams (9 oz) split pigeon peas (toor dal), toor dal, thoroughly washed

¼ teaspoon turmeric powder

1 medium tomato, chopped

2 green chilies, sliced

150-200 grams (5-9 oz) white radish, cut into 5 cm (2") long thick slices

1 medium onion cut into 2.5 cm (2") chunks

½ teaspoon thick tamarind paste

4 tablespoons Sambhar Powder (page 122)

Salt to taste

1 teaspoon mustard seeds

10-12 curry leaves

Method:

- Pressure-cook the split pigeon peas with turmeric powder, tomato, green chilies and radish.
- In a pot, boil the onion chunks in a cup of water till translucent. Do not overcook.
- Mix the sambhar powder with a tablespoon of water.
- Add the tamarind paste, salt and sambhar powder paste, to the cooked dal mixture.
- Adjust water for the required consistency.
- Bring to a rapid boil for 5-7 minutes.
- Heat oil in a small ladle, add mustard seeds and curry leaves, when they splutter turn off the heat and add this to the sambhar.
- Garnish with chopped coriander leaves. Serve hot with medu vada and/or idli.

Serves 6-8 people

Note: For the longest time, I used my mom's sambhar powder. Then after coming to the USA, we had gone to Udupi for a conference and we visited my first cousin there. We loved the sambhar that his wife made. I wanted the recipe, but like many women, she could only tell me the quantities of the ingredients, by showing them in her hand as "this much". I had to ask her to make a batch of sambhar powder and measured every "this much" ingredient in a measuring spoon, so I could write it down.

Upma

Ingredients

2 cups semolina (rava/sooji)

½ cup oil

2 teaspoons mustard seeds

2 sprigs curry leaves

1 tablespoon skinless split black gram (dhuli urad dal)

6-8 green chillies, finely chopped

2 medium onions, chopped

2.5 cm (1") piece ginger, grated or finely chopped

1 tablespoon salt

1-2 teaspoons sugar or as per taste

1 small tomato, finely chopped

½ cup peas (fresh or frozen)

Coriander leaves, chopped

Method:

- Dry roast the semolina on medium heat for 4-5 minutes and set aside.
- Heat the oil in a kadhai, add mustard seeds, curry leaves, urad dal, green chillies, onions and fry on medium flame till translucent.
- Add roasted semolina, grated ginger and fry till light beige in color. Add salt, sugar, tomato, peas and fry for 5 minutes.
- Add 6 cups of boiling water, mix well, lower the heat to minimum, cover with a lid and cook for 5-7 minutes till fairly dry and not sticky.
- Garnish with coriander leaves. Serve hot.

Serves 8-10

Chef's tip: Roasting of semolina is the key to achieving the right texture of upma. Do not rush while dry roasting as well as when roasting the onions.

Batata Vada

Ingredients

For the stuffing

1 kg (2.2lb) potatoes, boiled and peeled

14-15 green chilies

2.5 cm (1") piece ginger

½ cup coriander leaves, chopped

½ teaspoon turmeric powder

Salt to taste (approx. 2 teaspoon)

For the batter

200 grams (7 oz) gram flour

1 teaspoon chili powder

½ teaspoon turmeric powder

⅛ teaspoon baking soda

Salt to taste

Water, approx. 1¼ cups

Method:

For the potato ball stuffing

- Chop green chilies and ginger together in a chopper.
- Mash the boiled potatoes.
- Add green the chilies, ginger, coriander leaves, turmeric powder and salt to the mashed potatoes.
- Mix all ingredients well.
- Make golf sized balls and keep aside.

For the batter

- Mix all the dry ingredients of the batter together.
- Add the water slowly to make a batter, ensuring that it is free from lumps.
- Dip the potato balls in the batter one at a time.
- Deep fry the coated balls in hot oil on a medium high heat, till light brown.
- Serve hot with garlic chutney.

Makes 20 vadas

Note: My mom ate the batata vadas served at the stalls set up by the Shiv Sena, when they first started in Mumbai and figured out the recipe. I have been eating them since then. She had a knack of figuring out recipes, which I have inherited to some extent!

Chakli

Ingredients

2 cups rice flour

1 cup wheat flour

⅓ cup vegetable shortening, melted (I used Crisco/Dalda)

¼ teaspoon turmeric powder

Pinch of asafoetida

3 teaspoons chili powder

¾ teaspoon cumin seeds

1½ teaspoons sesame seeds

Salt to taste

Water (approx. 1⅓ cup)

Oil for frying

Method:

- Mix the rice flour, wheat flour, turmeric powder, asafoetida, chili powder, cumin seeds and sesame seeds together in a bowl.
- Add the melted vegetable shortening to the dry ingredients and knead into a soft dough using water.
- Make chaklis in the chakli mold on a wax paper.
- Pour about 5 cm (2") of oil in a shallow frying pan and heat it.
- Fry chaklis on a medium low heat till light golden brown.
- Drain onto a paper towel.
- When cool, store them in an airtight container.

Makes 30

Chef's Tip: The proportion of the Crisco is very important.

Note: These are the best chaklis that I have eaten and are thanks to my friend Swarup who taught me how to make them 19 years ago. I have shared her recipe with many people.

Corn Tikkis

Ingredients

500 grams (18 oz) corn kernels, ground

1 cup green capsicum, finely chopped

1 cup red capsicum, finely chopped

4-6 green chilies, finely chopped

1.5 cm (½") piece ginger, finely chopped or grated

1 cup coriander, finely chopped

1 cup onions, finely chopped

1 teaspoon cumin seeds

1 teaspoon coriander powder

1 teaspoon red chili powder

½ teaspoon chaat masala

1½ cups rice flour

Water for kneading

Oil for frying

Salt to taste

Method:

- In a bowl add the ground corn, green capsicum, red capsicum, green chilies, ginger, coriander, onions, cumin seeds, coriander powder, red chili powder and chaat masala.
- Add the rice flour and mix well.
- Gradually add approximately ¼ cup of water or as needed to form a dough-like consistency.
- Take a golf ball size of dough and flatten it on your palm. Make small tikkis/patties and deep fry the tikkis in hot oil on medium heat in frying pan, till golden brown.
- Serve hot with green chutney or ketchup.

Makes 20

Chef's Tip: You can use frozen corn kernels or fresh corn on the cob.

Note: We get a lot of corn in summer here in the USA. So, I had to experiment with a few recipes. This was one of them after a few trials.

Dal Vada

Ingredients

1 cup split Bengal gram (chana dal), soaked for 4-6 hours

½ cup skinless split black gram (dhuli urad dal), soaked for 4-6 hours

2 green chilies, chopped

6-7 curry leaves

½ teaspoon ginger, chopped

1 tablespoon coriander leaves, finely chopped

½ teaspoon cumin seeds

½ teaspoon turmeric powder

2 teaspoons red chili powder

1 teaspoon coriander seeds powder

1 teaspoon fennel seeds

1 onion, finely chopped

2 tablespoons rice flour

Oil for greasing

Method:

- Keep aside 2 tablespoons split Bengal gram and 1 tablespoon skinless split black gram to use later.
- Grind the rest of it coarsely.
- Add the green chilies, curry leaves, ginger, coriander leaves, cumin seeds, turmeric powder, red chilli powder, coriander powder, fennel seeds, onion, rice flour and the whole lentils that were kept aside.
- Add salt and mix well.
- Grease your palm with oil, take a small portion and make small flat patties, about 5 - 7 cms (2-3") in size.
- Heat oil in a deep fryer, fry the vada on both sides on medium heat till golden brown.
- Our crispy dal vadas are ready.

Serves 4

Note: A very common evening snack that my mom made for us when we returned from school in the evening. There are a lot of childhood memories connected with this recipe.

Fresh Salsa

Ingredients

4 Roma tomatoes, roughly chopped

2 jalapeno green chilies, roughly chopped

¼ medium onion, roughly chopped

⅛ green bell pepper, roughly chopped

1 large pod garlic, roughly chopped

¼ cup coriander leaves, roughly chopped

1 can (6 oz, 170 grams) tomato sauce

¼ cup white vinegar

Salt to taste

1 teaspoon sugar

Method:

- Chop the tomatoes, jalapenos, onion, green pepper, garlic and coriander leaves together in a food processor by pulsing it to avoid them getting pureed.
- Add the tomato sauce, white vinegar, salt to taste, sugar and mix well.
- Adjust salt and sugar as per taste.
- Serve with tortilla chips.

Serves 4-6

Note: This is one of those recipes that I figured out after eating it a few times in Mexican restaurants. I have shared this recipe with many of my friends and American colleagues who loved it. Of course, some of them had to decrease the jalapenos to suit their palate.

Kothimbir Bhajji

Ingredients

3 cups coriander leaves, chopped

¾ cup gram flour

Salt to taste

2 tablespoons Shinde Masala Powder (page 123)

⅛ teaspoon baking soda

¾ cup water, or as needed

Method:

- Mix all the ingredients and make a semi soft dough using water.
- Heat oil in a deep pan.
- Drop small balls of the dough in the hot oil and deep fry them on a medium heat. Serve hot.

Serves 3-4

Note: This is a great short cut and alternative to the Kothimbir vadi that is a traditional Maharashtrian recipe. When you're a working woman and a foodie, you have to come up with shortcuts without compromising on the taste.

Khandvi (Microwave)

Ingredients

1 cup gram flour

1 cup yogurt

2 cups water

Salt to taste

¼ teaspoon turmeric powder

Pinch asafoetida

2-3 tablespoons oil

1 teaspoon mustard seeds

1 teaspoon sesame seeds

7-8 curry leaves, finely chopped

Method:

- Blend gram flour, yogurt and water in a blender till it is smooth and without lumps. Transfer to a microwave safe bowl.
- Add salt, turmeric powder, asafoetida and oil. Mix well.
- Cook in microwave at the highest temperature for 2 minutes.
- Take it out and stir well. Make sure there are no lumps. Cook for 2 more minutes.
- Remove and stir again to ensure there are no lumps. Cook again for 2 more minutes.
- Take out and stir till smooth. Microwave for 1 more minute. Stir till smooth.
- While it is still hot, quickly spread it thinly on the counter or the back of a tray.
- When it is cold, cut into thin strips and make the khandvi into small rolls. Keep them on a dish.
- Heat oil, add mustard seeds, sesame seeds and curry leaves. When they splutter, pour them over the khandvi. Garnish with coriander leaves.

Serves 4-6

Note: I keep experimenting with microwave cooking. This is a microwave version of the traditional way of making khandvi. The skill lies in spreading the batter thinly on surfaces (I do it on my clean granite counter) and rolling them into rounds. Recently my newly married daughter-in-law (Morli) made this and I was super impressed with her cooking talent.

Samosa

Ingredients

For the stuffing

6 medium sized potatoes, boiled, peeled and cubed

½ cup green peas, boiled

1 teaspoon cumin seeds

8 green chilies, chopped

2 cm (¾") piece ginger, finely chopped

3 teaspoons coriander-cumin powder

1 teaspoon chili powder

½ teaspoon garam masala

1 teaspoon dry mango powder

Salt to taste

¼ cup chopped coriander leaves

For the dough

3 cups all-purpose flour

⅓ cup hot oil

¼ teaspoon carom seeds

Salt to taste

Method:

- Heat oil in a pan, add cumin seeds.
- When they splutter, add green chilies and ginger and fry for a few seconds.
- Add coriander-cumin powder, chilli powder, garam masala, dry mango powder and sauté well. Add the potatoes, salt, coriander leaves and mix well for 2 more minutes. Keep aside to cool.
- Knead the flour into a hard dough using approximately ¾ cup of water and let it rest for an hour.
- Make golf sized balls of the dough and roll each into a chapati.
- Cut each chapati into half. Stuff each portion with the potato stuffing, close the open edges to make a samosa and deep fry in hot oil on medium heat till evenly browned.
- Serve hot with green chutney.

Makes 25 samosas

Note: When we lived in India, we used to love the samosas that we got near our house. But we never got similar crisp samosas and the spicy stuffing combination here in the USA. So, here we go. Necessity is the mother of invention!

Seekh Kababs

Ingredients

450 grams (1lb) 85% lean ground turkey

1 medium onion, finely chopped

¼ cup finely chopped coriander leaves

2 teaspoons salt

½ teaspoon dry mango powder

2 tablespoons tandoori masala powder

2 teaspoons coriander powder

⅛ teaspoon ginger powder

⅛ teaspoon garlic powder

1 egg

¼ cup breadcrumbs

Method:

- Mix all the ingredients together to form a dough.
- Take a small ball of the dough and press it around a wooden skewer to make seekh kababs.
- Cook the seekh kababs in a grill pan on the stove top on medium high heat, rotating them periodically to evenly cook on all sides.
- Remove the seekh kababs from the skewers onto an aluminum foil lined sheet, sprinkle some water, cover with a foil and bake at 350°F (175°C) for 15 minutes.

Makes 9-10 skewers of seekh kababs

Note: I loved these kababs, when I had them at my friend, Dr. Rita Kaul's house. They were so delicious; I would have never believed they were made with ground turkey. She was kind enough to come to my house and teach me how to make them. Thanks Rita!

SFC (Shak's Fried Chicken)

Ingredients

12 pieces of chicken thighs or drumsticks, washed and with slits made in the meat

24 green chilies or as per taste

1 black cardamom

2.5 cm (1") piece ginger

8 flakes garlic

½ cup coriander leaves

10-15 peppercorns

1 teaspoon fennel seeds

4 cloves

5 cm (2") piece cinnamon

2 flakes star anise

2 pinches nutmeg

1 teaspoon cumin seeds

2 tablespoons lemon juice

2 eggs

Method:

- Grind together the green chilies, black cardamom, ginger, garlic, coriander leaves, peppercorns, fennel seeds, cloves, cinnamon, star anise, nutmeg and cumin seeds.
- Add ½ teaspoon turmeric powder, lime juice and salt to taste, to the ground masala paste.
- Marinate chicken pieces in the masala paste for 3-4 hours, or overnight in the fridge. Bring to room temperature 1 hour before frying.
- Dip each chicken piece in the beaten egg. Drain the excess egg, and deep fry in hot oil in a shallow pan (covered with a lid), on a medium-low heat till brown on one side.
- Turn the chicken pieces over and brown on the other side and cook till done.

Serves 4-5

Note: I've eaten this when I was growing up, and my mom made it. We just called it fried chicken. After coming to the USA, I compared this recipe with KFC and thought that my mom's fried chicken won hands down. Hence, I started calling it SFC (Shinde's/Shak's Fried Chicken).
My husband has suggested to me several times, that I should introduce this dish in a place next to a KFC outlet. I know I would be sued due to the amount of spiciness this dish has.

Shrimp or Prawn Pakora

Ingredients

1 cup fresh, small baby shrimps (or regular shrimps, chopped), thoroughly washed

1 cup gram flour

½ cup finely chopped onion

½ cup finely chopped coriander leaves

4 green chilies, finely chopped

1 teaspoon finely chopped ginger-garlic

Salt to taste

Method:

- Heat the oil in a deep fryer.
- Mix all the ingredients together, without adding any water. Add very little if needed.
- Drop small lime sized balls of the mixture in oil and fry evenly on all sides, on a medium high heat, to golden brown.
- Serve hot with any sauce of your choice or green chutney.

Serves 3-4

Tandoori Chicken

Ingredients

14 chicken drumsticks, skinned, washed and with slits made in the meat

For the marinade

7 tablespoons yogurt

½ teaspoon ginger powder

1 teaspoon garlic powder

3 teaspoons chili powder

½ teaspoon garam masala powder

3 teaspoons salt

7 teaspoons cumin seed powder

1 tablespoon oil

Few drops of red food color

Method:

- Mix all the ingredients for the marinade.
- Marinate the chicken for 3-4 hours.
- Grill the marinated chicken on the barbeque or broil in the oven at 500°F (260°C).
- Turn the chicken pieces over and broil on the other side till done.

Serves 5-6

Chef's Tips: You could use chicken wings too since they are smaller in size and go very well as an appetizer.

Note: Again, this is one more dish that had to be discovered to satisfy our palate for delicious and spicy Tandoori chicken in the USA.

Stuffed Mushrooms

Ingredients

900 grams (2 lb) mushrooms

1 cup breadcrumbs

½ cup Parmesan or Swiss cheese, grated

¼ cup butter, melted

2 tablespoons minced onions

½ teaspoon pepper powder

Salt to taste

Method:

- Clean the mushrooms and remove the stems.
- Chop half the stems and mix with the rest of the ingredients.
- Stuff the mushrooms and broil for 5-8 minutes in a toaster oven.

Serves 6-8

Note: Mushroom is an ingredient that people either love or hate. But this dish is liked by most people who hate mushrooms too.

Tuna Fish Cutlets

Ingredients

3 medium potatoes, boiled, peeled and mashed

1 (142 grams, 5oz) can tuna fish, water drained completely

Salt to taste

½ teaspoon black pepper powder

3-4 green chilies, finely chopped

1 teaspoon ginger-garlic paste

1 small onion, finely chopped

1 teaspoon coriander seeds powder

½ teaspoon garam masala

⅓ cup coriander leaves, finely chopped

1 egg

2 tablespoons water

⅓ cup breadcrumbs for coating

Method:

- In a bowl, mix the mashed potatoes with the tuna fish, salt, pepper powder, green chilies, ginger-garlic paste, onion, coriander powder, garam masala and coriander leaves.
- Mix well.
- Form into cutlets.
- Beat the egg with water.
- Dip each cutlet in the egg wash, coat well with breadcrumbs on all sides.
- Heat about 2.5 cm (1") of oil in a shallow pan, and fry the cutlets till golden brown on both sides on a medium-high heat.
- Serve hot with ketchup.

Makes 8-10 cutlets

Chef's Tips: Mash the potatoes well before adding the fish, otherwise the fish flakes will completely disintegrate. Once all the ingredients are added to the mashed potato, it should be mixed well only using a fork.

This is a quick and easy recipe inspired by the traditional fish cutlets where you take fresh fish and boil them with herbs and spices and shred them.

Broccoli Bake

Ingredients

450 grams (1lb) broccoli, cut into fine florets

1 red pepper

1 onion, chopped finely

¼ cup grated mozzarella cheese

For the sauce

3 eggs

1 cup of milk

2 tablespoons oil

4 tablespoons all-purpose flour

2 teaspoons salt

1 teaspoon black pepper powder

5 grams (.2 oz) baking powder

2 teaspoons dill, chopped, fresh or dry

Toppings

¼ cup mozzarella cheese, grated

½ cup cheddar cheese, grated

Method:

- Preheat oven to 350°F (approx. 177°C).
- Beat the eggs.
- Add all the ingredients for the sauce and mix well.
- Mix in all the vegetables, cheese and chopped onion well.
- Grease a baking dish and add chopped vegetables.
- Spread the mozzarella cheese on top.
- Pour the sauce over and sprinkle cheddar cheese on the top.
- Bake in a pre-heated oven for 30-40 minutes or till a toothpick comes clean.

Serves 4-6

Black Chana Chaat

Ingredients

1½ cups Black Bengal gram (kala chana), washed and soaked in water overnight

Salt to taste

½ teaspoon red chili powder

1 teaspoon Kashmiri chili powder

½ teaspoon coriander powder

1 teaspoon dried mango powder

½ teaspoon turmeric powder

½ teaspoon fennel seeds, coarsely powdered

2 teaspoons dried fenugreek leaves, crushed by hand

2-3 tablespoons oil

1 teaspoon cumin seeds

⅛ teaspoon asafoetida

2 cm (¾") piece ginger, grated or minced

2-3 green chilies, finely chopped

2 large tomatoes, grated or pureed

1 onion finely chopped

1 tomato, finely chopped

Coriander leaves, chopped

Method:

- Pressure cook the soaked Black Bengal gram till done with salt and approximately 3 cups of water.
- Mix together salt, chili powder, coriander powder, dried mango powder, turmeric, powdered fennel seeds, and crushed fenugreek leaves, adding a little water to make a paste.
- Heat oil in a pan, add cumin seeds and asafoetida.
- When they splutter, add ginger, green chilies and fry for a minute.
- Add the masala paste and cook for a minute. Add pureed tomatoes, lower the heat and cover with a lid and cook for 2-3 minutes stirring periodically.
- Drain the water from the cooked chana and add them to the pan.
- Keep stirring on a high heat and cook till dry.
- To serve, put a small quantity of chana in a bowl, add chopped onions, chopped tomatoes and lots of coriander leaves on top.
- Enjoy the chaat.

Serves 4-6

Spinach Balls

Ingredients

1 pkt. (280 grams, 10 oz) frozen, chopped spinach, thawed with the water squeezed out and drained

1 cup breadcrumbs

1 medium onion, chopped

2 eggs, beaten

½ stick butter, melted

¼ cup Parmesan cheese powder

½ teaspoon garlic salt

½ teaspoon pepper powder

¼ teaspoon carom seeds

Method:

- Combine all the ingredients together. Refrigerate for about 1 hour or longer.
- Roll into balls.
- Preheat oven to $350°F$ (approx. $175°C$).
- Bake on a cookie sheet for 20 minutes.

Serves 4-6

Kadhi Pakora

Ingredients

For the Pakoras

1 cup gram flour

¼ teaspoon baking powder

Salt, as per your taste

½ teaspoon red chili powder

¼ teaspoon turmeric powder

½ cup water

1 onion, finely chopped

2 green chilies, finely chopped

½ teaspoon coriander seeds, crushed

1 tablespoon ghee

For the Kadhi

1 cup sour curd

1 lemon (if you are not using sour curd)

¼ cup gram flour

Salt to taste

½ -1 teaspoon red chili powder

½ teaspoon turmeric powder

1 liter (2 pints) water

For the Tadka

1 teaspoon mustard seeds

7 - 8 curry leaves

1 teaspoon cumin seeds

½ teaspoon fenugreek seeds

1.5 cm (½") piece ginger

2-3 green chilies

¼ teaspoon asafoetida

½ teaspoon coriander seeds

2 dried red chilies, broken

¼ cup oil

Method:

For the Pakoras

- Make a batter with the gram flour and water, add the salt, red chili powder and turmeric to the gram flour batter, then add onion, green chilies and coriander seeds.
- Lastly add the ghee and mix well.
- Heat oil and deep fry lime sized pakoras and keep aside.

For the Kadhi

- Mix all the ingredients for the kadhi in a bowl, making sure that there are no lumps in the mixture.
- In a large, deep pan heat the oil and add all the ingredients for the tadka, in the same order as mentioned in the list.
- Then add the kadhi mixture and bring it to a boil on high heat, continuously stirring until it comes to a boil.
- Lower the heat to medium and keep boiling for 15-20 minutes, stirring intermittently.
- Garnish with chopped coriander leaves and keep aside.
- Just before serving, add pakoras and bring to one boil.

Serves 4-6

Chef's Tips: Always add the ghee at the end when making the pakora batter. While making the kadhi, it is very important to keep stirring until it starts to boil. Save any left-over pakoras and kadhi separately and add the pakoras to warm kadhi a few minutes before serving.

Zucchini Mushroom Stir Fry

Ingredients

2 tablespoons oil

450 grams (1 lb) zucchini, cubed

225 grams (½ lb) mushrooms, quartered

2 green chilies, finely chopped

1 cup sliced onions

½ teaspoon ginger powder

½ teaspoon black pepper powder

Method:

- Heat oil in a stir fry pan, add chopped green chilies, onions and fry for 1-2 minutes.
- Add zucchini, mushrooms, ginger powder, pepper powder and stir fry on high heat till dry.
- Add salt and stir fry for 2 more minutes.
- Serve hot as a side dish with any rice dish and curry.

Serves 4

Tondli Garlic Fry

Ingredients

450 grams (1 lb) small gherkins (tondli)

12-14 flakes garlic, crushed

7 green chilies, slit lengthwise

Salt to taste

Method:

- Wash the gherkins well, crush them, keeping them intact. Add salt and keep them aside for an hour.
- Heat oil in a pan, add crushed garlic and green chilies. Sauté till garlic turns light brown. Add gherkins, fry for 1-2 minutes on high heat.
- Sprinkle 1 tablespoon of water, cover with a lid, lower the heat to medium-low and cook till done, stirring periodically.
- Stir fry few more minutes, uncovered till the gherkins become brown in color.
- Serve hot with chapatis.

Serves 3-4

Baingan Bhartha

Ingredients

1 large eggplant
(approx. 450 grams or 1 lb)
1 teaspoon cumin seeds
4-5 green chilies, finely chopped
2 medium onions, chopped
1 small tomato, chopped
½ teaspoon turmeric powder
½ teaspoon chili powder
1 teaspoon coriander-cumin powder
½ cup frozen peas
½ cup oil
Salt to taste

Method:

- Apply oil all over the eggplant and broil/roast in an oven or an air fryer till the skin is charred. Cover and keep aside.
- When cool, remove the skin and chop or mash the eggplant roughly to obtain a crushed pulp.
- Heat oil in a pan, add cumin seeds.
- When they splutter, add green chilies, onion and sauté on medium heat, covered, until the onions are translucent.
- Add tomatoes, cover and cook till soft making sure it doesn't burn at the bottom.
- Add turmeric powder, coriander-cumin powder, peas and sauté for 2-3 more minutes.
- Add the crushed eggplant pulp, salt and sauté for 2-3 minutes.
- Garnish with chopped coriander leaves and serve hot with chapatis.

Serves 3-4

Chef's Tips: Line a tray with aluminum foil to keep the oiled eggplant so it's a lesser mess to clean up. Chop the broiled eggplant into a rough pulp. It should not be mushy or a fine paste. So, avoid using a blender for this step.

Capsicum Aloo Sabzi

Ingredients

2 pinches of asafoetida

1 teaspoon cumin seeds

1 medium onion, finely chopped

2 medium sized potatoes, cut into 2.5 cm (1") cubes

1 teaspoon ginger-garlic paste

½ teaspoon turmeric powder

1 teaspoon red chili powder

2 teaspoons coriander seeds powder

1 medium tomato, finely chopped

2 medium capsicums, cut into 2.5 cm (1") cubes

½ teaspoon garam masala powder

2-3 tablespoons chopped coriander leaves

Method:

- Heat oil. Add asafoetida and cumin seeds. When the cumin seeds splutter add the onion.
- Sauté till pinkish to light brown in color. Add potato and sauté for 2-3 minutes.
- Cover with a lid and cook till onions are brown.
- Add ginger-garlic paste and sauté for 30 seconds, till the raw smell goes.
- Add turmeric powder, red chili powder, coriander seeds powder and sauté well for a minute.
- Add the tomato and mix well. Add salt to taste and cook, covered with a lid.
- Add capsicum and mix well. Add garam masala powder, coriander leaves and mix well, cover and cook for 4-5 minutes.
- Serve hot.

Serves 4

Black-eyed Peas Curry

Ingredients

1 cup black-eyed peas

1 large potato, cut into 5 cm (2") cubes

2 medium onions, finely chopped

½ cup coriander leaves, chopped

2 teaspoons ginger-garlic paste

2 medium tomatoes, finely chopped

½ teaspoon turmeric powder

1 tablespoon Malavni masala or any mix masala that you use

Salt to taste

1 teaspoon garam masala powder

8 cardamom pods, peeled and powdered

½ cup oil

Method:

- Pressure cook the black-eyed peas with 3 cups of water till done.
- Heat the oil and fry the onions on a medium heat till light brown.
- Add the ginger-garlic paste, coriander leaves and fry till the raw smell goes away.
- Add tomatoes and fry till almost dry.
- Add turmeric powder, masala mix and potatoes and fry for 2-3 minutes.
- Add half the salt to taste and 1 cup of water, cover with a lid and cook till almost done.
- Add the boiled black-eyed peas, the remaining salt to taste, garam masala, cardamom powder and boil for 5-6 minutes.
- Garnish with coriander leaves.
- Serve hot with rice.

Serves 4

Chef's Tips: Kothimbir bhajji or fresh baby shrimp bhajji goes well with this curry.

Cabbage-Chana Dal Subzi

Ingredients

900 grams (2 lb) cabbage, chopped

½ cup split Bengal gram (chana dal), soaked in water for an hour

1 large onion, chopped

1 medium tomato, chopped

1 teaspoon mustard seeds

2 sprigs curry leaves

½ teaspoon turmeric powder

1 teaspoon red chili powder

1 teaspoon coriander-cumin powder

1 teaspoon garam masala powder

Salt to taste

¼ cup oil

Coriander leaves to garnish

Method:

- Heat ¼ cup oil in a sauce pan.
- Add mustard seeds and curry leaves.
- When they splutter, add onions and fry on a medium heat till pink in color.
- Add split Bengal gram, turmeric powder and salt to taste.
- Cover with a lid and cook till half done.
- Add cabbage, tomatoes, red chili powder, coriander-cumin powder and garam masala powder.
- Cook till done.
- Garnish with chopped coriander leaves.
- Serve hot with chapatis.

Serves 4

Mahki Dal

Ingredients

1 cup skinless split black gram (dhuli urad dal)

½ cup split Bengal gram (chana dal)

2.5 cm (1") piece ginger, finely chopped

6 pods garlic, finely chopped

½ teaspoon turmeric powder

Salt to taste

1 teaspoon cumin seeds

1 small onion, finely chopped

1 teaspoon chili powder

1 teaspoon garam masala powder

Coriander leaves for garnishing

⅓ cup oil

Method:

- Wash both the grams together thoroughly.
- Cook them in a pressure cooker with 4 cups of water, ginger, garlic, turmeric powder and salt. Cook till soft but not broken. Heat oil in a pan, add cumin seeds.
- When they splutter, add onions and fry till brown on a medium heat. Add chili powder and fry for 1-2 minutes.
- Pour over the cooked gram, adjust the consistency, add garam masala and boil for 4-5 minutes.
- Garnish with chopped coriander leaves. Serve hot with rotis, parathas or rice.

Serves 4

Note: This is another recipe that my mother-in-law learnt while living in Delhi. Usually, Mahki Dal is made with black urad dal. But she used white urad dal, without the skin, which tastes different from the regular Mahki Dal. For me, this is Maa (Mother/Aai) ki Dal.

Chole

Ingredients

½ kg (18 oz) chickpeas (Kabuli chana), washed and soaked in water overnight

½ teaspoon turmeric powder

Salt to taste

2 medium (approx. ¼ kg, 9 oz) onions, sliced

2.5 cm (1") piece ginger

8 flakes garlic

1 tablespoon chili powder

2 teaspoons dry mango powder

4 teaspoons coriander-cumin powder

1 teaspoon garam masala

2 teaspoons pomegranate seeds, roasted and powdered

Oil for frying

Method:

- Pressure-cook the soaked chickpeas with 4 glasses of water, salt to taste and turmeric powder till done.
- Fry the onions in a little oil till dark brown (almost black).
- Grind the onions together with the ginger and garlic.
- Fry the ground paste in 6-8 tablespoons oil till dry.
- Add the chili powder, dry mango powder, coriander-cumin powder, garam masala and fry till there is a nice aroma.
- Add the cooked chickpeas, pomegranate seeds powder and water for the desired consistency and boil.
- Garnish with chopped coriander leaves.

Serves 4-5

Note: My in-laws were living in Delhi several years ago, before I came into their family. I learnt this most tasty chole dish from my mother-in-law and modified it a bit by using dry mango powder and pomegranate seeds powder to get the dark color. She used tamarind juice, to be added on the top, as per individual taste for sourness.

Palak Paneer

Method:

- Cook spinach with half a cup of water in a microwave dish for 7-8 minutes, stirring in between.
- Blend cooked spinach in a food processor to a coarse texture.
- Heat the oil in a medium sized, non-stick pan on high heat.
- Once oil is hot, add in the minced onions, cook until light golden brown for about 5 minutes.
- Add the ginger and garlic and mix. Cook for another 4-5 minutes.
- Add the tomatoes, cover and cook till the oil separates from the mixture.
- Keep stirring frequently as the masala (onion, tomato, ginger and garlic mixture) tends to burn very fast.
- Once the masala is prepared, mix and add the garam masala, cumin powder, coriander seeds powder, salt, chili powder and turmeric powder. Mix well and cook for 3-5 minutes.
- Add in the mashed spinach.
- Add in the cream or milk. Mix and cook for another few minutes.
- Add dried fenugreek leaves.
- Add the cottage cheese cubes to the spinach.
- Mix gently and serve hot.
- Enjoy with naan, chapati or paratha.

Serves 4

Ingredients

570 grams (20 oz) fresh spinach

200 grams (7 oz) cottage cheese (paneer), cubed

4 tablespoons oil

2 medium onions, minced

2.5 cm (1") piece ginger, minced

7 pods garlic, minced

½-¾ cup water

1 Roma tomato or 4 tablespoons crushed tomatoes

1 teaspoon garam masala powder

1 teaspoon cumin powder

2 teaspoons coriander seeds powder

1 teaspoon red chili powder

½ teaspoon turmeric powder

Salt to taste

4 tablespoons heavy whipping cream or ¼ cup evaporated milk

1 teaspoon dried fenugreek leaves

Corn Capsicum Masala

Ingredients

300 grams (10½ oz) corn, boiled in a microwave for 5 minutes

2 medium capsicums, cut into 2.5 cm (1") cubes

½ teaspoon cumin seeds

2 medium onions, chopped

1 teaspoon ginger-garlic paste

¼ cup crushed tomatoes

1 teaspoon red chili powder

½ teaspoon turmeric powder

Salt to taste

1 tablespoon coriander powder

1 teaspoon cumin powder

1 teaspoon garam masala powder

¼ cup evaporated milk or 1 tablespoon heavy cream

¼ cup oil

Method:

- Heat the oil in a medium sized sauce pan, add the cumin seeds. When the cumin seeds splutter, add onions, fry till pink.

- Add the ginger-garlic paste and fry till golden brown. Add tomatoes, red chili, turmeric powder, salt, coriander, cumin powder and stir fry till oil leaves the sides of the vessel. Add capsicum and cook for 3-4 minutes.

- Add ½ cup water, corn, and cover and cook for 4-5 minutes. Add garam masala, milk or cream and cook for another 2-3 minutes till desired consistency is reached.

- Garnish with chopped coriander leaves. Serve hot with chapatis.

Serves 4

Matar Paneer

Ingredients

- 2 onions, roughly chopped
- 2-3 green chilies, roughly chopped
- 1.5 cm (½") piece ginger, roughly chopped
- 4-5 garlic pods, roughly chopped
- 3 tomatoes, roughly chopped
- 2 tablespoons cashews, soaked in a little water
- 4 tablespoons oil
- 1 teaspoon cumin seeds
- 1 teaspoon red chili powder
- 1 tablespoon cashew paste
- ½ teaspoon turmeric powder
- 2 teaspoons coriander powder
- 1 teaspoon cumin powder
- ½ teaspoon sugar
- 400 grams (14 oz) fresh peas
- 1 teaspoon garam masala
- 200 grams (7 oz) cottage cheese (paneer), cubed

Method:

- Heat 1 tablespoon oil in a pan. Add roughly chopped onions, green chilies, ginger, garlic and fry till the onions are translucent and soft. Do not brown them.
- At this stage, add tomatoes, salt and cook covered, till oil leaves the sides and tomatoes are mushy. Keep stirring periodically.
- Grind to a fine paste, when cooled down. Grind soaked cashews to a fine paste.
- Heat remaining 3 tablespoons oil in a pan, add cumin seeds.
- When they splutter, add chili powder and fry on a low heat for a minute.
- Add cashew paste and fry till the red color deepens. Add the ground paste, turmeric powder and fry till oil leaves the sides, on low medium heat.
- Add coriander, cumin powder and sugar and fry for some more time.
- Add green peas and cook covered till soft. Add garam masala, water for desired consistency, cottage cheese cubes, cover and cook for 4-5 minutes on medium heat. Boil until you get the desired consistency.
- Garnish with chopped coriander leaves.

Serves 4-5

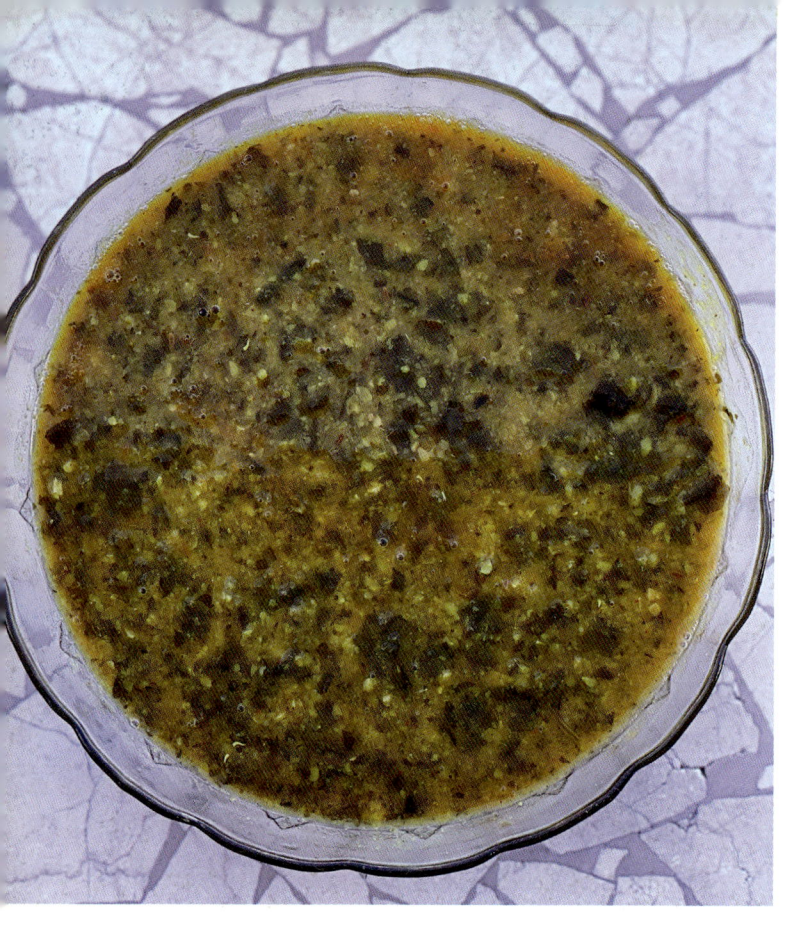

Dal Palak

Ingredients

1 cup split pigeon peas (toor dal), thoroughly washed

225-280 grams (8-10 oz) spinach, fresh or frozen, chopped

½ teaspoon turmeric powder

2.5 cm (1") piece ginger, grated

1 medium tomato, chopped

½ teaspoon tamarind paste

Salt to taste

½ tablespoon cumin seeds

1 tablespoon garlic, finely chopped

½ tablespoon, or to taste, chili powder

2 tablespoons oil

Method:

- Pressure cook split pigeon peas with 3 cups of water, spinach, turmeric powder, ginger and chopped tomato.
- In a pan, heat oil, add cumin seeds, garlic. When they splutter, add chili powder and fry for a minute.
- Add the cooked dal mixture, salt, tamarind paste and boil for 4-5 minutes.
- Adjust water for required consistency. Serve hot with rice.

Serves 4

Eggplant Bhaaji

Ingredients

450 grams (1 lb) long and thin Chinese eggplant

8-10 flakes garlic

1 small tomato

¼ teaspoon turmeric powder

1 teaspoon chili powder

1 teaspoon salt

1 tablespoon jaggery or brown sugar

2 tablespoons oil

Method:

- Heat 2 tablespoons oil in a non-stick pan.
- Add crushed garlic and sauté till golden. Add all the remaining ingredients and stir fry on medium heat till done.
- Garnish with 2 tablespoons grated fresh coconut. Serve hot with chapatis.

Serves 4

Chef's Tips: While cooking, do not cover with a lid. Do not cook until mushy, it should be slightly on the crisp side.

Gobi Capsicum Masala

Ingredients

300 grams (10 -11 oz) cauliflower florets
2-3 red chilies
½ teaspoon cumin seeds
½ teaspoon ginger, chopped
½ teaspoon garlic, chopped
1 medium onion, sliced
Salt to taste
2-3 green chilies, slit (optional)
1 tablespoon tomato ketchup
½ teaspoon coriander powder
½ teaspoon red chili powder
1 capsicum, green or any color, cut into 2.5 cm (1") cubes
3-4 tablespoons coriander leaves, chopped
¼ teaspoon black pepper, crushed
1 teaspoon lemon juice
½ cup oil

Method:

- Cut the cauliflower into florets and par boil them in a little water to which salt and turmeric are added. Drain and keep aside.
- Add oil to the pan, when it heats up, put in dry red chilies, cumin seeds, ginger, garlic, onions and a little salt.
- Sauté all the ingredients well until they turn translucent.
- Add green chilies, tomato ketchup and sauté well till the tomato mixture dries off. Add turmeric powder, coriander powder, red chili powder and sauté well for 1 more minute.
- Add capsicum, boiled cauliflower florets. Sauté well until the florets are nicely coated by the spice mixture.
- Add coriander leaves and freshly crushed black pepper. Sauté the ingredients well. Add lemon juice and stir over high heat for few minutes.
- Serve hot with rotis, chapatis, naans or rice.

Serves 8

Karela (Bitter Gourd) Sabzi

Ingredients

Approximately 300 grams (10 oz) bitter gourd cut into thin rounds, salted for 15-20 minutes and the liquid squeezed out

3 medium onions, thickly sliced

½ teaspoon mustard seeds

½ teaspoon cumin seeds

½ teaspoon fennel seeds

½ teaspoon black caraway seeds

1 small tomato, pureed

½ teaspoon turmeric powder

1 teaspoon chili powder

1 teaspoon coriander seeds powder

1 teaspoon dry mango powder

Salt to taste

½ cup oil

Method:

- In a frying pan, add ½ cup oil and fry the bitter gourd till golden brown.
- Remove and fry onions in the same oil till they are pink in color.
- Remove and keep them aside with the bitter gourd.
- In the same pan, leave approx. 2 tablespoons of oil and remove any excess oil.
- Add the mustard seeds, cumin seeds, fennel seeds and black caraway seeds.
- When they splutter, add the tomato puree, 1 teaspoon salt and fry till dry on a medium heat.
- Add all masala powders and fry for 2-3 minutes. Add fried bitter gourd and onions and mix well.
- Cover with a lid and cook on a low heat for 5-7 minutes.
- Garnish with coriander leaves.

Serves 3-4

Mushroom Masala

Ingredients

340 grams (12 oz) mushrooms, quartered
1 bay leaf
1 large onion, finely chopped
1 tablespoon ginger-garlic paste
4 tablespoons tomato puree
¼ cup cashews, soaked in water for about half an hour, ground to a fine paste
1 teaspoon chili powder
¼ teaspoon turmeric powder
1 teaspoon coriander powder
1 teaspoon garam masala powder
Salt to taste
4 cardamom pods, peeled and powdered
Coriander leaves, chopped, to garnish
½ teaspoon sugar
⅓ cup oil

Method:

- Heat the oil in a medium saucepan. Add bay leaf, onions and fry till golden brown.
- Add ginger-garlic paste and sauté for 1 more minute.
- Add tomato puree and fry till dry.
- Add the turmeric, chili, coriander and garam masala powders and sauté for 2-3 minutes.
- Add cashew paste and sauté till oil leaves the sides of the vessel.
- Add 1 cup of water, cover and boil for 1-2 minutes.
- Add mushrooms, salt, sugar, cardamom powder, cover and cook for 5 minutes.
- Adjust consistency and salt and garnish with coriander leaves.

Serves 4

Palak Mushroom

Ingredients

570 grams (20 oz) packet of fresh spinach

225 grams (8 oz) white mushrooms

10-12 flakes of garlic

7 green chilies

1 teaspoon turmeric powder

2 teaspoons coriander-cumin powder

1½ teaspoons salt to taste

¼ cup oil

Method:

- Heat the oil in a medium sized pan, add chopped garlic and chopped green chilies. Fry till garlic is pink in color.
- Add turmeric powder and coriander-cumin powder and sauté for 1 more minute on medium heat.
- Add chopped spinach and cook till wilted (without covering with a lid).
- Add salt and quartered mushrooms.
- Cook for 7-8 minutes, till done.

Serves 4

Stuffed Okra
(Bhindi)

Ingredients

900 grams (2 lb) small okra, washed and dried

2 medium potatoes, sliced thick, with a slit on each slice

14-16 green chilies

1 cup coriander with stems

20 flakes garlic

Salt to taste

4 teaspoons coriander-cumin powder

1 teaspoon turmeric powder

2 medium sized tomatoes

Method:

- Slit the okra in the center.
- Grind the green chilies, coriander leaves, tomatoes and garlic to a fine paste.
- Add salt, coriander-cumin powder, turmeric powder.
- Stuff the okras and potatoes with this mixture.
- Add some oil in an oven proof tray.
- Line the potatoes on the tray, and add the okras on top.
- Add ½ cup water mixed with remaining masala.
- Cover with foil and bake for approximately 1 hour till the okra is cooked.
- Remove foil and bake further till dry.

Serves 3-4

Sprouted Moong Curry

Ingredients

- 1 tablespoon oil
- ½ teaspoon mustard seeds
- ½ teaspoon fenugreek seeds
- 20 peppercorns (or to taste)
- 2 tablespoons coriander seeds
- 10 dry red Byadgi chilies (or to taste)
- 1 cup shredded coconut
- 2.5 cm (1") piece of cinnamon
- 2 cloves
- Approx. 2½ cups water
- 1 pinch asafoetida
- 8-10 curry leaves
- ½ teaspoon turmeric powder
- 1 cup sprouted green gram (sprouted moong), soaked overnight and sprouted, makes 4 cups
- 2 medium tomatoes, chopped
- Salt to taste
- Coriander leaves, chopped for garnish
- Lime/Lemon juice to taste

Method:

- Heat 1 teaspoon of the oil in a skillet on medium heat.
- Add in the mustard seeds and allow them to pop. Add in the fenugreek seeds, peppercorns and the coriander seeds. Roast for 30-40 seconds, and add in the dry red chilies. Stir constantly and cook till the spices give out a nice aroma and the chilies turn a darker color.
- Turn off the heat and add the shredded coconut and keep stirring in the hot pan for a few minutes.
- Add cinnamon and cloves to the roasted mixture and grind to a fine paste and keep aside. Add water a little at a time to make a smooth paste.
- In a pan, add in the asafoetida, curry leaves and the turmeric powder, add the sprouted green gram, ground coconut mixture, balance of the water, salt and tomatoes. Mix well. Cover and cook till done.
- Garnish with lemon/lime juice and coriander leaves to serve.
- Serve hot with rice or chapatis.

Serves 6-8

Note: This is an Udupi dish that was usually made on festival days. Hence, no onion or garlic is used in this recipe.

Vegetable Korma

Ingredients

- 2 medium onions, roughly chopped
- 4 tablespoons fresh grated coconut
- 7-8 green chilies
- 1.25 cm (½") piece ginger
- 1.25 cm (½") cup coriander leaves
- 4 flakes garlic
- 1 tablespoon coriander seeds
- 1 teaspoon cumin seeds
- ¼ teaspoon pepper
- 4 cloves
- 2.5 cm (1") piece cinnamon
- Pinch of nutmeg
- 2 florets star anise
- 1 teaspoon poppy seeds soaked in 2 tablespoons water for 10 minutes
- 1 teaspoon fennel seeds
- 1 medium tomato
- 1 black cardamom pod
- ⅛ cup broken cashew pieces
- ½ teaspoon turmeric powder
- 1 large potato, cubed
- 450 grams (1 lb) cauliflower, cut into florets
- 450 grams (16 oz) packet, frozen mixed vegetables
- Salt to taste
- 1 cup water
- 1 green pepper, cubed
- ½ cup oil for frying

Method:

- Grind together the onions, coconut, green chilies, ginger, coriander leaves, garlic, coriander seeds, cumin seeds, pepper, cinnamon, cloves, nutmeg, star anise, poppy seeds, fennel seeds, tomato and black cardamom.
- In a large pan heat the oil, fry the cashew pieces and keep aside.
- In the remaining oil, fry the ground paste till golden brown, add turmeric powder and fry for 2-3 minutes more on a medium low heat.
- Add the potato and fry for 4-5 minutes more. Add cauliflower and fry for few more minutes. Cover and cook till three-fourths done.
- Add the frozen mixed vegetables, salt to taste and fry for a few more minutes. Add water, green peppers and cook till done.
- Garnish with chopped coriander leaves.

Serves 7-8

White Peas (Vatana) Curry

Ingredients

¼ kg white peas (vatana), soaked overnight

7-8 red Byadgi chilies

¼ teaspoon black pepper

2 teaspoons coriander seeds

1 cup freshly grated coconut

4 cloves

2.5 cm (1") piece of cinnamon

2 medium potatoes, peeled and cubed

½ teaspoon turmeric powder

Salt to taste (2 teaspoons)

1 tomato, finely chopped

1 teaspoon mustard seeds

10-12 curry leaves

2 teaspoons oil

Method:

- Pressure cook the white peas with 4 cups of water. Do not overcook.
- Heat ½ teaspoon oil in a pan and roast red chilies, pepper and coriander seeds.
- Grind this together with coconut. When almost fine, add cloves and cinnamon. Grind to a fine paste.
- In a large vessel, boil potatoes with turmeric powder and half the salt, till almost cooked.
- Add tomato, ground masala, remaining salt and cooked vatana and boil for 4-5 minutes.
- Heat the remaining oil in a small tempering pan, add mustard seeds and curry leaves.
- When they splutter add them to the boiling curry, cover with the lid and turn off the heat.
- Serve hot with rice.

Serves 4-6

Note: This is another Udupi dish that has no onion or garlic in it. So, can be made on auspicious occasions.

Whole Moong Dal

Ingredients

1 cup whole green gram, thoroughly washed

½ teaspoon turmeric powder

4 tablespoons oil

1 teaspoon mustard seeds

8-10 curry leaves

1 teaspoon cumin seeds

1 tablespoon garlic, minced

1-2 tablespoons Shinde Masala Powder (page 123)

Salt to taste

Coriander leaves, chopped for garnishing

Method:

- Add turmeric powder, 3 cups of water and a drizzle of oil into the green gram, and cook in a pressure cooker till soft.
- Heat the oil in a medium saucepan or kadhai, add mustard seeds.
- When they splutter, lower the heat to very low and add curry leaves, cumin seeds and garlic. Stir fry for a few seconds.
- Add Shinde masala powder and stir fry for 10-15 seconds. Add cooked green gram mixture, salt and boil for 5-7 minutes on a medium low heat.
- Garnish with coriander leaves.

Serves 4-5

Chef's Tips: Make sure to keep the heat very low after the mustard seeds splutter to avoid burning the garlic and masala powder.

Amma's Chicken Curry

Ingredients

½ kg (8 oz) onions, thinly sliced

2 teaspoons ginger-garlic paste

1 teaspoon turmeric powder

2 kg (4½lb) chicken, cut into 5 cm (2") cubes

Salt to taste

2 medium tomatoes, chopped

1 can coconut milk

½ teaspoon black pepper

8 teaspoons coriander seeds

2 teaspoons fennel seeds

2 teaspoons poppy seeds

42 Byadgi chilies (dry red chilies) or as per your taste

8 cloves

1 teaspoon cumin seeds

5 cm (2") piece cinnamon

½ teaspoon fresh nutmeg, grated

4 florets of star anise

2 pods black cardamom

2 teaspoons mace

8 pods garlic

Method:

- Dry roast pepper, coriander seeds, fennel seeds and poppy seeds.
- Dry roast red chilies separately.
- Grind all the roasted ingredients with the cloves, cumin seeds, cinnamon, nutmeg, star anise, black cardamom, mace and garlic into a fine paste using water as required.
- Fry sliced onions in butter or ghee till golden brown. Add ginger garlic paste and fry for 1 more minute.
- Add turmeric powder, chicken, salt to taste, tomatoes and let it seal (changes color and turns opaque). Add ground masala paste, 2 cups water, lower the heat to low setting, cover and cook until done.
- Add coconut milk, water to desired consistency and boil for 3-4 minutes.
- Garnish with chopped coriander leaves. Serve hot with rice or bread (pav).

Serves 8

Chef's Tips: Byadgi chilies are mild and give more color than spiciness to the curry.

Note: This is a very sentimental dish for me. During my courtship days with my husband, my to be in-laws were so impressed with this recipe that, I think they agreed to our inter-caste marriage, almost 45 years ago, only because of this dish!!

Bhuna Chicken

Ingredients

450 grams (1 lb) chicken

1 teaspoon cumin seeds

2 bay leaves

4 dried red chilies, cut to pieces

8 cloves

2 pods black cardamom

4 pods green cardamom

5 cm (2") stick cinnamon

4 medium onions, sliced thinly

2 tablespoons ginger-garlic paste

½ teaspoon turmeric powder

2 teaspoons cumin powder

2 teaspoons coriander powder

2 teaspoons red chili powder

2 teaspoons garam masala powder

1 teaspoon tandoori masala powder (optional)

1 tablespoon ghee

Method:

- Heat oil in a non-stick pan. Add cumin seeds, bay leaves and dried red chili pieces.
- When cumin seeds begin to splutter, add cloves, black cardamom, green cardamom, cinnamon and sauté for 1-2 minutes.
- Add onions and fry till pink. Add ginger-garlic paste and sauté till raw smell goes. Add turmeric, chili, cumin, coriander and garam masala powders and sauté for 2-3 minutes more. Add chicken, salt to taste and cook covered till done. Add ghee and fry for 1 more minute.
- Garnish with chopped coriander leaves. Serve hot.

Serves 4-6

Chef's Tips: You could powder the pieces of the garam masala if whole pieces are not preferred while eating. The tandoori masala powder is added to get the reddish bhuna color.

Chicken 65

Ingredients

1.8 kg (4 lb) boneless chicken thighs, cut into 5 cm (2") pieces

8 teaspoons yogurt

1 teaspoon ginger powder

1 teaspoon garlic powder

½ tablespoon garam masala powder

4 teaspoons chili powder

2 teaspoons salt

¼ teaspoon red food coloring

3 tablespoons corn flour

3 tablespoons all-purpose flour (maida)

1 egg

2 teaspoons mustard seeds

1 teaspoon cumin seeds

8 sprigs curry leaves

Method:

- Mix all the ingredients well and marinate chicken pieces in the mixture.
- Keep in the refrigerator for 4 hours or overnight.
- Deep fry in oil on high heat and remove onto a plate.
- For the tempering, in a small pan add mustard seeds, cumin seeds and curry leaves. When they splutter, turn off the stove and add the fried chicken pieces and mix well.
- Serve hot as an appetizer or as a side dish with pulao and raita.

Serves 7-8

Note: My friend Swarup made this and I loved it. Again, she was only able to give me the ingredients and I had to come up with the measurements to match the taste of her recipe. I think cooking is an art for most women, but for me it's a combination of art and science as described by our friend Sudhir.

Chettinad Mutton Curry

Ingredients

900 grams (2 lb) mutton (goat's meat), cut into 2" cubes

4 small onions, chopped

1 tablespoon ginger-garlic paste

2 tomatoes, chopped

1 teaspoon turmeric powder

Salt to taste

1 cup water

4 tablespoons oil

5 cm (2") stick cinnamon

½ teaspoon fennel seeds

1 teaspoon Kashmiri red chili powder

5 cm (2") cinnamon sticks

8 cloves

1 full star anise

4 pods of black cardamom

1 teaspoon fennel seeds

1 teaspoon cumin seeds

1 teaspoon peppercorns

8 dry red chilies

1½ tablespoons coriander seeds

½ cup desiccated dry coconut

Method:

- Roast cinnamon stick, cloves, star anise, cardamom, fennel seeds, cumin seeds, peppercorns, dry red chilies, coriander seeds and desiccated coconut on a medium heat and grind it to a smooth powder. (This is the recipe for Chettinad mutton masala powder.)

- In a sauce pan, heat the oil, temper it with cinnamon sticks and fennel seeds.

- Add onions and sauté well till golden brown in color. Add ginger garlic paste and fry it until raw smell goes. Add tomatoes and sauté until mushy.

- Add turmeric powder, freshly ground masala powder, Kashmiri red chili powder and sauté for 2 more minutes. Add the mutton pieces, salt to taste and mix well with the masala. Add water and pressure cook until done or alternately slow cook until done.

- Garnish with chopped coriander leaves. Serve hot with roti, naan or parathas.

Serves 6

Note: We love this dish which is served at a local restaurant. This is one of the recipes that I figured out, and after a few trials came up with this recipe.

Chicken Biryani

Ingredients

5 cm (2") piece mace
¼ teaspoon peppercorns
4 pods green cardamom
4 pods black cardamom
4 cloves
5 cm (2") stick cinnamon
2 flakes star anise
1½ teaspoons black cumin seeds
4 bay leaves
900 grams (2 lb) chicken, cut into 7-10 cm (3-4") pieces
2 tablespoons red chili powder
1 tablespoon ginger garlic paste
¼ teaspoon turmeric powder
1 teaspoon cumin powder
1 tablespoon coriander powder
Salt to taste
½ cup yogurt
1 cup chopped coriander leaves
A handful of mint leaves, chopped
½ cup fried onions
2-4 green chilies or as per taste
½ cup oil
2 tablespoons lime juice
2 cups Basmati rice, washed and soaked for 2 hours
8 cups of water
2 pinches of saffron
¼ cup ghee
¼ cup cashews
2-3 tablespoons raisins

Method:

- Powder mace, peppercorns, 2 pods each of green and black cardamom, cloves, cinnamon stick, star anise and ½ teaspoon black cumin seeds.
- Take a bowl, add chicken pieces, powdered garam masala, red chili powder, ginger-garlic paste, turmeric powder, coriander powder, cumin powder, yogurt, coriander leaves, mint leaves, fried onions, green chilies, lime juice, half of the oil, and mix well. Marinate the chicken pieces overnight in this mixture, in the fridge.
- In a pan, bring water to boil.
- Add 2 bay leaves, remaining ½ teaspoon black cumin seeds, salt and 1 teaspoon oil.
- Add the rice to the boiling water and cook till three-fourths done.
- Drain the water and keep the rice aside.

- Soak saffron in 2 tablespoons water and keep aside.
- Heat a pan on medium heat, add the remaining oil, ghee and fry the cashews and raisins and drain out.
- In the same oil, add the remaining whole spices 5 cm cinnamon stick, 2 bay leaves, 2 pods each of black and green cardamom and fry for half a minute.
- Add ½ teaspoon black cumin seeds and allow them to sizzle.
- Add the marinated chicken, mix well and cover and cook till three-fourths done.
- Preheat the oven to 250°F (120°C).
- Coat an oven proof dish with a little oil.
- Add the chicken and then add a layer of rice, a layer of cashews and raisins, coriander and saffron. Drizzle some oil on top.
- Cover with an air tight lid or aluminum foil and bake for 1 hour.
- Allow it to sit on the counter for 5-7 minutes and serve hot with any raita.

Serves 8

Chicken Handi

Ingredients

1 kg (2.2 lb) chicken thighs with bones, cut into 5 cm (2") cubes

1.5 cm (½") piece ginger

4 flakes garlic

2 green chilies

¼ cup coriander leaves

4 tablespoons yogurt

½ teaspoon turmeric powder

½ cup oil

400 grams (14 oz) finely chopped onion

2 large tomatoes, finely chopped or pureed

4 teaspoons Malavni masala or any masala mix that you use

1 teaspoon garam masala

2 teaspoons fennel seeds, roasted and powdered

Method:

- Grind ginger, garlic, chilies and coriander leaves into a fine paste.
- Marinate the chicken pieces in a mixture of yogurt, turmeric powder, salt and ground green paste for 1 hour.
- Fry onions in oil till golden brown.
- Add tomatoes and fry till oil leaves the sides.
- Add marinated chicken and fry till sealed.
- Add Malavni masala, garam masala and ¼ cup water and cook till almost done.
- Add fennel powder and cook till done.
- Garnish with coriander leaves and serve hot with rotis/naans/parathas.

Serves 4

Chicken-Liver Palak Masala

Ingredients

680 grams (24 oz) spinach (fresh or frozen), chopped

225 grams (½ lb) eggplant

6-8 tablespoons butter

6 small onions (approx. 600 grams, 20 oz)

3 tablespoons ginger-garlic paste

1 teaspoon ground green chilies (optional)

1 teaspoon turmeric powder

3 small tomatoes, chopped

1.5 kg (3.3 lb) chicken liver and gizzards mixed, cut into pieces

3 tablespoons mutton masala

1 teaspoon garam masala powder

Salt to taste

Method:

- Boil spinach and eggplant till soft.
- When cooled, mash it or run it through a food processor. Do not puree it.
- Fry sliced onions in butter till golden brown.
- Add green chilies, ginger-garlic paste and fry. Add washed gizzards, turmeric powder, salt and fry for a few minutes more.
- Add tomatoes, 2 tablespoons mutton masala, fry for a few minutes and pressure cook for 3-4 whistles.
- Once the cooker cools down, add liver, remaining 1 tablespoon mutton masala, garam masala, boiled spinach and eggplant.
- Cook till liver is done. Serve hot with roti, naan or paratha.

Serves 6-7

Chef's Tips: You could use mutton liver (kaleji) and make the same dish.

Note: My mom used to make this dish, but my family didn't like it much because of the smell that was imparted by the liver or gizzards. Once, I added 1 cup of left-over baingan bhartha to the spinach and they all loved it that day. So, the secret ingredient here is the eggplant.

Crab Curry

Ingredients

- 3 King crab legs or about 700 grams (1½ lb) whole crabs
- ⅓ cup oil
- 1 large onion
- 3 medium potatoes, quartered
- 1½ teaspoons poppy seeds
- 2 teaspoons mustard seeds
- 2 teaspoons black cumin seeds
- 2 teaspoons fennel seeds
- 1 teaspoon black caraway seeds
- 1 teaspoon fenugreek seeds
- 3 medium tomatoes
- 9 large flakes garlic
- 3.75 cm (1½") piece ginger
- ¾ cup coriander leaves
- 3 teaspoons chili powder
- 3 teaspoons Kashmiri chili powder
- 3 teaspoons coriander powder
- 3 teaspoons cumin powder
- ¾ teaspoon turmeric powder

Method:

- Roast poppy seeds, mustard seeds, black cumin seeds, fenugreek and black caraway seeds. Powder and keep aside.
- Boil quartered onion in the microwave, covered for 2 minutes.
- Grind it with tomatoes, garlic, ginger and coriander leaves
- Heat oil and fry the ground paste till the raw smell goes away.
- Add chili powder, Kashmiri chili powder or paprika (for color), coriander powder, cumin powder, turmeric powder and fry till dry.
- Add the powdered masala, salt, crab legs and approx. 1½ cups of water, cover and cook for 5-6 minutes till it starts to boil. Add potatoes, water as needed for desired consistency, cover and cook for about 1 hour, stirring periodically.

Serves 4

Note: My friend Neela Chowdhary taught me this recipe since I love crabs. Thanks Neela.

Green Chicken

Ingredients

- 1 kg (2.2 lb) chicken with bones, cut into pieces
- 2 teaspoons coriander seeds
- ½ teaspoon cumin seeds
- 1 teaspoon fennel seeds
- 1 teaspoon sesame seeds
- 1 teaspoon poppy seeds
- 4 cloves
- 5 cm (2") piece cinnamon
- 10-15 peppercorns
- 16 green chilies
- 1 cup coriander leaves
- 1.5 cm (½") piece ginger
- 6-8 flakes garlic
- 2 tablespoons dry coconut powder
- 1 pod black cardamom
- 2 pinches nutmeg powder
- 1 piece mace
- 1 floret star anise
- 2 large onions (approx. 400 grams or 14 oz)
- ½ teaspoon turmeric powder
- Salt to taste
- ½ cup water

Method:

- Dry roast the coriander seeds, cumin seeds, fennel seeds, sesame seeds, poppy seeds, cloves, cinnamon and peppercorns.
- Grind the roasted spices with green chilies, coriander leaves, piece of ginger, garlic, dry coconut powder, black cardamom, nutmeg, star anise and mace.
- Fry the chopped onions in butter or oil until brown, on medium heat.
- Add the turmeric powder, ground paste and fry till dry.
- Add chicken pieces and fry till sealed.
- Add salt to taste, water and cook on low heat, covered, till done.
- Serve hot.

Serves 4-6

Kheema

Ingredients

1 kg (2.2. lb) ground meat (goat or lamb)

2 onions (approx. 350 grams or 10 oz), finely chopped

1 teaspoon turmeric powder

Salt to taste

¼ cup Shinde Masala (page 123) or any masala mix that you use

½ cup peas

Grind into a fine paste

2.5 cm (1") piece ginger

8 flakes garlic

1 medium tomato

½ cup coriander leaves

2 tablespoons dry coconut

1 teaspoon fennel seeds

10-15 peppercorns

1 pod black cardamom

4 pinches nutmeg

7 cloves

5 cm (2") piece cinnamon

2 florets star anise

Method:

- Fry the chopped onions in oil till golden brown on a medium heat.
- Add the ground paste, ground meat and fry till it crumbles. Add turmeric powder, salt and fry till dry. Add the Shinde masala and fry till oil leaves the sides.
- Add peas, 2-3 cups of water and boil for 5-6minutes.
- Garnish with coriander leaves.
- Serve hot with roti or bread (pav).

Serves 4

Chef's Tips: You could use any ground meat. But it tastes better if the ground meat is chunky and not powdery.

Also, be mindful when adding salt, since the Shinde masala has a fair amount of salt in it.

Lamb Pepper Fry

Ingredients

- 1 tablespoon oil
- 1 tablespoon butter
- 2 cloves
- 5 cm (2") piece cinnamon
- 1 pod black cardamom
- 2 pods green cardamom
- ¼ teaspoon black cumin seeds
- ¼ teaspoon cumin seeds
- 1 large onion, chopped
- ¼ teaspoon turmeric powder
- 1 tablespoon ginger garlic paste
- 450 grams (1 lb) lamb/ goat meat, cubed
- 4 pods garlic
- ½ teaspoon cumin seeds
- 8 peppercorns
- 1 teaspoon coriander powder
- ½ teaspoon cumin powder
- 1 teaspoon red chili powder
- 1 bunch chopped coriander
- 10 curry leaves
- Salt to taste
- 3 green chilies, slit

Method:

- In a heavy bottom pan add the oil. When the oil is hot, add cloves, cinnamon, black cardamom, green cardamom and black cumin seeds.
- When they splutter, add cumin seeds and chopped onions, and cook till onions are pink in color. Add turmeric and ginger garlic paste and fry till the raw smell goes. Add nicely cleaned cubes of lamb or mutton, add a little water and cook till meat is tender.
- Make sure that the lamb is fully cooked as we are not going to cook this lamb in a gravy or anything else.
- Pound garlic, cumin seeds and peppercorns in a mortar and pestle.
- Melt the butter in a broader pan, add the pounded garlic/peppercorns/cumin seeds mixture and fry for a minute.
- Add green chili and curry leaves and fry for a few seconds. Add red chili powder, cumin powder, coriander powder and fry for 1-2 minutes.
- Add lamb, fry till water dries up. Add the chopped coriander to garnish and a little lime juice to taste.

Serves 3-4

Chef's Tips: Use a broader pan, so that the moisture evaporates quickly.

Mutton Noval Kol Curry

Ingredients

1 kg (2.2 lb) mutton, cubed
½ kg (1.1 lb) kohlrabi (novalkol), cut into large chunks
4 medium onions, thinly sliced
5 cm (2") piece ginger, finely chopped or grated
8 flakes garlic
2 medium tomatoes
1 teaspoon turmeric powder
2 tablespoons mutton masala or any masala mix
1 teaspoon garam masala
½ cup oil

Method:

- Sauté onions and finely chopped garlic in oil.
- Add turmeric, mutton, salt, grated ginger, tomatoes and brown the meat.
- Add mutton masala, 2 cups of water and cook in slow cooker for about 3 hours or on a low heat till three-fourths done.
- Add kohlrabi, garam masala and cook for 2 more hours in slow cooker or till the meat is tender.
- Garnish with chopped coriander leaves.

Serves 6

Chef's Tips: Preferably do not pressure cook.

Pomfret Fish Curry

Ingredients

1 cup fresh coconut, grated

2 tablespoons coriander seeds

15 dry Byadgi red chilies

3 tablespoons coconut oil

1 medium onion, finely chopped

2.5 cm (1") piece ginger, finely chopped

¾ teaspoon turmeric powder

5-6 kokums or 1 teaspoon tamarind pulp

Salt to taste

450 grams (2 lb) pomfret, sliced into 7-8 pieces

Method:

- Clean and wash the fish.
- Grind the coconut, coriander seeds and the chilies to a fine paste gradually adding 1 cup of water.
- Heat a deep bottom vessel and heat the coconut oil.
- When the aroma of the coconut oil fills the air, add the onion and the ginger and sauté till the onion is light pink and soft.
- Add the ground coconut masala, turmeric powder, salt and kokum and 2 cups of water to make the gravy and bring to a boil.
- After you boil the gravy check the salt, spice and sour taste, once you adjust these flavors to your liking, add the fish and let it cook on a slow heat for 10 minutes or till the fish is done.
- Serve hot with rice.

Serves 4

Chef's Tips: Always adjust the flavor of the curry before you add the fish, because it becomes difficult to do it after the fish is added as the fish meat is delicate and the pieces might break.

Shrimp Sukka

Method:

- Dry roast coriander seeds, cumin seeds, mustard seeds, fenugreek seeds, sliced onion, garlic and red chilies and keep aside.
- When cooled, blend them into a fine paste.
- Dry roast grated coconut in the same pan and keep aside.
- Heat the oil in a pan, add mustard seeds.
- When they splutter, add curry leaves and chopped onions and fry till the onions are pink in color.
- Add shrimps and sauté for a few minutes.
- Add turmeric powder, salt and cook for 2-3 minutes.
- Add ground masala paste, tamarind paste, mix well, cover with a lid and cook for 4-5 minutes.
- Add roasted coconut and mix well.
- Sauté till the water dries upto the desired consistency.
- Garnish with coriander leaves.
- Serve hot with chapatis.

Serves 4

Ingredients

2 teaspoons coriander seeds
2 teaspoons cumin seeds
½ teaspoon mustard seeds
¼ teaspoon fenugreek seeds
½ medium onion, sliced
4 pods garlic
10-12 dry red Byadgi chilies
1 cup fresh grated coconut
1 tablespoon oil
½ teaspoon mustard seeds
1 medium onion, chopped
450 grams (1 lb) shrimp/prawns, shelled and de-veined
¼ teaspoon turmeric powder
Salt to taste
½ teaspoon tamarind paste
Coriander leaves to garnish

Shrimp Capsicum Masala

Ingredients

9 tablespoons fresh coconut

¾ cup coriander leaves

6 green chilies

4 cm (1½") piece ginger

10-12 flakes garlic

3 small tomatoes

3 large red onions, finely chopped

¾ teaspoon turmeric powder

6 teaspoons Malavni masala or any masala mix

½ cup oil

1.5 kg (approx. 3 lb) small shrimps

1½ large green peppers, cubed

Salt to taste

½ cup water

Coriander leaves to garnish

Method:

- Grind together coconut, coriander leaves, green chilies, ginger, garlic and tomatoes and keep aside.
- Heat the oil in a pan, fry the coarsely chopped onions till pinkish brown in color.
- Add ground paste, turmeric powder and fry till dry. Add Malavni masala, shrimps, green pepper, and fry for a few minutes till shrimps become opaque.
- Add salt, ½ cup of water and cook till it starts boiling. Adjust the curry to desired consistency for eating with chapatis or rice.
- Garnish with chopped coriander leaves.

Serves 7-8

Shrimp Curry (Shinde Style)

Ingredients

1.25 cm (½") piece ginger

8 flakes garlic

4 tablespoons dry coconut powder

½ cup coriander leaves

2 medium tomatoes

450 grams (1 lb) onions, finely chopped

½ teaspoon turmeric powder

4-5 tablespoons Shinde Masala (page 123)

900 grams (2lb) small size shrimps

½ cup oil

Salt to taste

Method:

- Grind together ginger, garlic, coconut powder, coriander leaves and tomatoes into a fine paste.
- Fry onions in oil till golden brown.
- Add turmeric powder, ground paste and fry till dry.
- Add Shinde masala and fry on a medium heat till oil leaves the sides.
- Add washed shrimps and fry for 3-4 minutes.
- Add salt as needed, 3-4 cups of water depending on required consistency and boil for 3-4 minutes.
- Serve hot with rice.

Serves 7-8

Chef's Tips: Be mindful when adding salt, since the Shinde masala has a fair amount of salt in it.

Mutton Rogan Josh

Ingredients

1 kg (2.2 lb) lamb/goat meat, cubed
2 teaspoons coriander seeds
1½ teaspoons poppy seeds
2 teaspoons grated dry coconut
1 tablespoon cashew nuts
5-6 cloves
15-20 peppercorns
7 pods green cardamom
10 flakes of garlic
5 cm (2") piece ginger
½ cup oil
½ kg (1.1 lb) onions, finely chopped
¼ cup yogurt
½ teaspoon garam masala
Salt to taste
¼ kg (9 oz) tomatoes, pureed or 40 grams (1½ oz) tomato paste
2 teaspoons chili powder
½ teaspoon turmeric powder

Method:

- Dry roast coriander seeds, poppy seeds, grated dry coconut, cashew nuts, cloves, pepper corns and green cardamoms
- Grind the roasted spices with garlic and ginger.
- Fry chopped onions in oil till golden brown.
- Add chili powder, turmeric powder and fry till the ghee leaves the sides.
- Add yogurt, tomato and ground paste, and fry for 3-4 minutes.
- Add mutton, garam masala powder, salt and fry till dry.
- Add 2 cups of water and cook till tender.
- Garnish with finely chopped coriander leaves.

Serves 6

Chicken Manchow Soup

Ingredients

2 tablespoons oil

3 tablespoons ginger-green chilies, crushed

10-15 cloves of chopped garlic

¼ cup assorted bell peppers, chopped

⅓ cup green cabbage, chopped

3 cups chicken stock

2 tablespoons light soy sauce

Salt and pepper as required

1 can (140-170 grams, 5-6 oz) cooked chicken breast

2 tablespoons corn starch

1 egg

3 tablespoons chopped coriander leaves

½ chicken stock cube optional

½ cup noodles

Method:

- Shallow fry the noodles in the oil until crisp and keep aside.
- In the same oil add crushed ginger-green chilies, garlic, chopped vegetables and stir fry them.
- Then add the chicken stock, soy sauce, salt, pepper and boil on high heat.
- Shred the chicken breast and add it to the boiling soup.
- Add corn starch slurry as a thickener.
- Beat an egg and add it to the soup.
- Finally, add coriander leaves and delicious hot chicken Manchow soup is ready to serve!

Serves 4

Chili Chicken (Indo-Chinese)

Ingredients

800 grams (1.5 lb) boneless chicken
2 tablespoons oil
¾ teaspoon white pepper powder
¾ teaspoon sugar
1 egg
½ tablespoon dark soy sauce +
½ tablespoon regular soy sauce
for marinating
½ tablespoon dark soy sauce +
1 tablespoon regular soy sauce
for the gravy
12 green chilies (4 finely chopped and 8 slit)
12 pods garlic, finely chopped
1½ cups (1 can) chicken stock
½ cup water
4 tablespoons corn starch
(1½ tablespoons for marination +
2½ tablespoons for gravy)

Method:

- Marinate the chicken pieces in a mixture of egg, salt, soya sauce and cornstarch for 20 minutes.
- Deep fry chicken in hot oil on high heat.
- Heat 2 tablespoons of oil in a wok and fry the garlic and green chilies for 1 minute.
- Add chicken stock or water and bring it to a boil.
- Add sugar, white pepper powder, salt and soya sauce.
- Add fried chicken pieces and boil for 3-4 minutes.
- Add corn starch dissolved in water, stirring continuously.
- Garnish with chopped spring onions.

Serves 4

Fried Rice

Ingredients

2 cups rice, washed

½ cup oil

½" piece ginger, finely chopped

2 spring onions, green parts for garnish

½ cup shredded cabbage

½ cup chopped carrots

½ cup peas

2 tablespoons soy sauce

Salt to taste

Method:

- Parboil rice, drain and keep aside.
- Heat oil, add ginger and onions and fry for 2-3 minutes.
- Add cabbage, carrots and peas and fry till just tender.
- Add salt, soy sauce and the rice.
- Stir fry till cooked and well blended.
- Garnish with spring onion greens.
- Serve hot.

Serves 4

Banana Choc-chip Bread

Ingredients

1 egg

3-4 ripe bananas, mashed

2 cups flour

1 cup sugar (adjust to taste)

¼ cup oil

1 teaspoon vanilla

½ teaspoon baking soda

½ teaspoon baking powder

½ teaspoon cinnamon powder

¼ teaspoon nutmeg powder

½ - ¾ cup chocolate chips, (or chopped nuts)

Method:

- Preheat the oven to 350°F.
- Beat egg in a large mixing bowl.
- Add bananas and mash well.
- Mix the rest of the ingredients well.
- Add ½ - ¾ cup chocolate chips, (or chopped nuts instead).
- Mix lightly.
- Grease a loaf pan or 22.5 x 27.5 cm (9 x 11") pan.
- Pour the batter in it.
- Bake for about 1 hour till done (the time varies with different ovens).

Serves 4

Note: Many years ago, when we were new in the USA, I learnt to bake from my American colleagues. This was the first dish that I made. I mastered it and my children grew up eating it frequently. Best use of over ripe bananas.

Carrot Halwa

Ingredients

900 grams (2 lb) carrots, finely shredded

¼ cup sugar

½ cup milk powder

1 can condensed milk (400 grams, 14 oz)

1 can evaporated milk (340 grams, 12 oz)

2 tablespoons ghee

2 tablespoons cashew nuts, chopped

2 tablespoons raisins

½ teaspoon, cardamom powder

Sliced almonds and pistachios to garnish

Method:

- Soak the raisins in some water.
- In a microwave safe, tall bowl, mix the carrots with evaporated milk, milk powder, condensed milk and sugar.
- Mix well and microwave for 10 minutes.
- Remove from microwave, mix well and microwave for another 10 minutes.
- Remove from microwave, mix well and microwave for 5 more minutes.
- Add the cardamom powder and mix well.
- Heat ghee in a small pan and add cashews and raisins, fry them for a minute.
- Add this to the halwa and mix well.
- Garnish with pistachios and sliced almonds.

Serves 7-8

Doodhi (Bottle Gourd) Halwa

Ingredients

900 grams (2 lb) grated bottle gourd, (no seeds)

2 tablespoons ghee

3 cups milk

1 cup milk powder

1 cup sugar

2 tablespoons raisins

2 tablespoons chopped cashews

½ teaspoon cardamom powder

Method:

- Heat ghee in a microwave and add grated bottle gourd, and cook for 2 minutes.
- Mix well and cook for 2 more minutes. Add milk and cook for 4 minutes.
- Repeat Steps 2 and 3, twice, mixing well each time. Add milk powder, microwave for 4 minutes.
- Repeat Step 5 twice, mixing well each time. Add sugar and cook for 2 minutes.
- Repeat Step 7 until the mixture becomes dry. Add raisins, cashew nuts, cardamom powder, and heat for 1 minute.
- Serve hot or cold as per taste.

Serves 4

Chef's Tips: If you want to make barfi, keep cooking until dry. Pat the mixture on a greased tray and let it cool. Cut into squares and serve as barfi.

Date and Nut Roll

Ingredients

340 grams (12 oz) chopped dates

¼ cup each, cashew nuts, pistachios, almonds, walnuts, chopped

1 teaspoon poppy seeds

½ teaspoon cardamom powder

½ teaspoon nutmeg optional

2 teaspoons ghee

Method:

- Grind dates in a food processor.
- Heat 1 teaspoon ghee in a non-stick pan and roast chopped nuts on a medium heat for 3-4 minutes.
- Remove and keep aside.
- Add 1 more teaspoon ghee in the same pan and roast poppy seeds on a low heat for 2 minutes.
- Now add ground dates mixture and mix well for 2-3 minutes.
- Add roasted nuts, cardamom powder and mix well till it forms into a lump.
- Turn off the heat and let the mixture cool for 4-5 minutes.
- Make 2-3 log rolls out of the mixture, wrap tightly in a foil and refrigerate for an hour.
- Slice and store the slices in an airtight container.

Serves 6-8

Pista Barfi

Ingredients

¾ cup milk

¾ stick unsalted butter

1 cup sugar

113 grams (4 oz) plain cream cheese

7-8 pods green cardamom, powdered

¾ cup dry non-fat milk powder

¾ cup unsalted pistachios, powdered

¾ cup unsalted almonds, powdered

Method:

- Cook milk, butter and sugar uncovered in a microwave, for 7-8 minutes till the mixture is boiling and bubbly.
- Remove from the microwave and add cream cheese and powdered green cardamom to the mixture.
- Add dry non-fat milk powder, and powdered pistachios and almonds.
- Cook uncovered in the microwave for 3-4 minutes.
- Remove from the microwave and mix well, and cook again for 2 minutes.
- Repeat this step until ghee leaves the sides or the mixture forms into a dough.
- Grease a tray with ghee and pour this mixture in the tray. Garnish with sliced nuts of your choice and let it set.
- Cut into pieces of the desired size, when cool.

Serves 8-10

Chef's Tips: Take a small spoonful of the mixture. If you are able to form it into a ball, it's done.

Ribbon Jell-O

Ingredients

Jell-O Layer

1 small box (3 oz/ 85 gm) cherry Jell-O
1 small box (3 oz/ 85 gm) orange Jell-O
1 small box (3 oz/ 85 gm) lime Jell-O
1 small box (3 oz/ 85 gm) pineapple Jell-O

White Mixture

2 cup milk
1 cup sugar
2 teaspoons vanilla
½ liter (1 pint, 16 oz) sour cream
2 envelopes (Knox) unflavored gelatin, dissolved in ½ cup cold water

Method:

White Mixture

- Add gelatin to cold water. Mix well and let stand.
- Boil milk in microwave.
- Add sugar and gelatin water. Let it cool for 5-7 minutes.
- Add this mixture slowly to the sour cream. Add vanilla and whisk well. Do not refrigerate.

Jell-O

1. Boil 1 cup water. Stir in cherry Jell-O. Add ½ cup cold water. Cool.

To make the finished Ribbon Jell-O

1. Pour the cherry Jell-O in a 30 x 22 cm (approx. 13"x 9") pan.
2. Refrigerate till set.
3. Put 1½ cups of the white mixture on top of the Jell-O and let it set in refrigerator for approximately one hour.
4. Repeat with other Jell-O mixtures, alternating with the white mixture and letting set really well (approximately one hour) between each layer.
5. Keep in the refrigerator till ready to serve.

Serves 10-12

Note: This is a beautiful looking dessert. It looks like a difficult recipe and all-day work. But it can be easily done, when cooking for a party, while cooking several other dishes. It looks intimidating, but is easy to do and tastes delicious. You could use different colored Jell-O, in your order of color preference, based on the theme of the party.

Rava Kesari

Ingredients

2 tablespoons ghee
5 cashew nuts, split in half
1 tablespoon raisins
½ cup semolina
1 cup water
¾ cup sugar
2 pinches of saffron soaked in 2 tablespoons water
¼ cup ghee
¼ teaspoon cardamom powder

Method:

- Heat ghee in a pan. Fry cashews and raisins on a low heat, till they plump up to a golden brown. Remove and keep aside.
- In the same pan, in the remaining ghee, add semolina and roast on a low heat for 5 minutes till aromatic. Keep aside.
- Boil 1 cup of water in the same pan, add roasted semolina, mix well and cook on a low heat till water is absorbed. Make sure the mixture has no lumps.
- Add sugar and mix well. Once sugar dissolves, add saffron water and mix well. Add ¼ cup ghee and mix well.
- Cover and simmer for 2 minutes.
- Add roasted cashew nuts, raisins and cardamom powder and mix well till the sheera starts separating from the pan.
- Serve hot.

Serves 2-3

Mango-Coconut Barfi

Ingredients

1 teaspoon ghee/desi ghee

1 cup coconut powder or fresh/frozen shredded coconut

1 cup milk

½ cup milk powder

¼ cup almonds (blended and separated into almond meal and small pieces by straining)

½ cup mango pulp

3 tablespoons sugar (or as per taste)

Method:

- Set a wide, non-stick, shallow pan on low-medium heat.
- Warm ghee in the pan.
- Add coconut powder and mix with the ghee. Roast for 30-40 seconds while mixing continuously.
- Add milk and stir occasionally till the milk dries up.
- Sprinkle milk powder and mix thoroughly.
- Add almond meal and one-third of the almond pieces. Mix well.
- Roast this mix for a few minutes until it becomes dry.
- Add mango pulp. Keep stirring and roast at high heat.
- Add sugar and keep roasting till all the moisture is dried up.
- Mix in all the lumps together. Switch off the heat.
- Let the mixture cool for a minute and then transfer to a greased square or rectangular tray.
- Mark cuts for the barfi pieces in the mix. Cover the plate with cling wrap and refrigerate for 2 hours.
- Store the cut pieces in the fridge.
- Enjoy homemade mango coconut barfi!

Serves 7-8

Note: Do not use coconut flour!

Chai Masala

Ingredients

25 grams (approx. 1 oz) green cardamom

5 black cardamoms

25 grams (approx. 1 oz) cloves

50 grams (approx. 2 oz) cinnamon sticks

½ teaspoon black pepper corns

1¼ teaspoons fennel seeds

100 grams (approx. 4 oz) ginger powder

1¼ teaspoons fresh nutmeg powder

Method:

- Roast all the ingredients except ginger powder and nutmeg powder.
- Remove and keep aside to cool.
- Turn off the stove and add ginger powder, nutmeg powder and roast in a hot pan.
- Powder the cooled ingredients and mix with ginger powder and nutmeg powder.
- Store in a dry container.

Kadai Masala Powder

Ingredients

3 tablespoons coriander seeds

1 tablespoon cumin seeds

1 tablespoon peppercorns

1 tablespoon fennel seeds

8-9 Kashmiri chilies

Method:

- Dry roast and grind all the ingredients into a coarse powder and store in an air tight container.

Sambhar Powder

Ingredients

25 red chilies (Byadgi)

4 tablespoons coriander seeds

2 tablespoons split Bengal gram (chana dal),

1 tablespoon skinless split black gram (dhuli urad dal),

½ tablespoon cumin seeds

1 teaspoon fenugreek seeds

1 teaspoon black peppercorns

1 teaspoon mustard seeds

6-8 sprigs curry leaves

½ teaspoon asafoetida powder

Method:

- Roast each of the ingredients separately in a few drops of oil.
- When cooled, powder and store in an air tight container.

Shinde Masala

Ingredients

½ kg (1.1 lb) red chili powder

450 grams (1 lb) salt

200 grams (7 oz) coriander seeds powder

125 grams (4.4 oz) cumin seeds powder

100 grams (3.5 oz) coconut powder

100 grams (3.5 oz) garlic powder

50 grams (1.8 oz) turmeric powder

Method:

- Mix all the ingredients together well and store in an air tight container.
- Use wherever it is mentioned in the recipe.

Measurements

1 cup = 250 gms (9 oz) = 200 ml

1 tablespoons = 15 ml

American and Indian Equivalents of Ingredients

English	Hindi	English	Hindi
All-purpose flour	Maida	Dried fenugreek leaves	Kasuri methi
Asafoetida	Hing	Dry mango powder	Amchur
Bay leaf	Tejpatta	Fennel seeds	Saunf
Bengal gram, split	Chana dal	Fenugreek seeds	Methi
Black caraway seeds	Kalonji	Gram flour	Besan
Black gram, skinless split	Dhuli urad dal	Mace	Javitri
Black gram, split	Urad dal	Mint	Pudina
Caraway seeds	Shahjeera	Mixture of spices	Masala
Cardamom	Elaichi	Mustard seeds	Rai
Carom seeds	Ajwain	Nutmeg	Jaiphal
Cashews	Kaju	Pigeon peas, split	Toor dal
Chickpeas	Kabuli Chana	Pomegranate seeds	Anardana
Cinnamon	Dalchini	Poppy seeds	Khuskhus
Clarified butter	Ghee	Raisins	Kishmish
Cloves	Lavang	Saffron	Kesar
Coriander seeds	Dhania	Semolina	Sooji
Coriander-cumin (seeds) powder	Dhaniajeera	Sesame seeds	Til
		Star anise	Chakriphool
Cumin seeds	Jeera	Tamarind	Imli